K. HAWES

JUNE 1980

LNER Album

Volume Three

A typical scene from the halcyon days of the LNER in the few years preceding World War II, with Gresley Class V2 three-cylinder 2-6-2 No 4813 attacking the gradient out of Kings Cross at Belle Isle on the second part of the 4pm Newcastle express on April 22, 1939. *E R Wethersett, Ian Allan Library*

LNER Album

Volume Three

BRIAN STEPHENSON

LONDON

IAN ALLAN LTD

First published 1976

ISBN 0 7110 0669 5

Published by Ian Allan Ltd, Shepperton, Surrey, and printed in the United Kingdom by Ian Allan Printing Ltd

Introduction

This third Album of LNER pictures has been produced in answer to all those readers of the two previous volumes who wrote to me suggesting that I might be persuaded into compiling a third. To all of these readers who gave me such encouragement and who have seen that the first two volumes have both run to a third impression I say Thank you!

I must also express my gratitude to the following photographers who have given me complete freedom to use their work in this book: C R L Coles, J G Dewing, L Hanson, F R Hebron, T G Hepburn, E E Smith and J P Wilson. To N Fields for the photographs by the late R D Pollard, to S W Stevens-Stratten for making available the prints of LNER road vehicles, to the Real Photographs Company Ltd for the pictures by the late H Gordon Tidey and finally to J L Smith of Lens of Sutton for the work of various anonymous photographers in his collection. The remaining photographs come from the publisher's own files. Lastly my wife has been the usual stern critic of prints and layout.

Thank you!

January 1976 *BWLS*

No 4419

QUEEN OF SCOTS

ABOVE: The most numerous class of express engines inherited by the LNER at the grouping in 1923 were the Ivatt Class C1 Atlantics of the GNR. Here No 3300 makes a fine sight as it heads a Newcastle-Kings Cross express over Langley water troughs about 1930. *F R Hebron*

UPPER LEFT: In 1923 Gresley fitted Class C1 4-4-2 No 4419 with a booster engine on its trailing axle to assist in accelerating from stops on awkward gradients. In fitting the booster the main frames were lengthened at the footplate end and a more commodious cab fitted. No 4419 is seen with booster in operation climbing Holloway bank with the 11.20am Kings Cross-Edinburgh Pullman in 1927. *F R Hebron*

LOWER LEFT: Class C1 Atlantic No 3280 comes bowling down from Stoke Tunnel towards Grantham at Saltersford with the down "Queen of Scots" Pullman from Kings Cross to Glasgow about 1936. Ninety-one of these engines were built to the standard pattern between 1902 and 1910 and all were later fitted with Robinson 32-element superheaters by Gresley. *T G Hepburn*

L N E R
3990

The pioneer British Atlantic, Ivatt Class C2 4-4-2 No 3990 *Henry Oakley* built by the GNR at Doncaster in 1898, departs from Kings Cross with the 1.45pm Cambridge train in February 1925. This class comprised 21 engines built in 1898-1903.
F R Hebron

ABOVE: In 1915 Gresley rebuilt standard Class C1 Atlantic No 3279 with four cylinders and Walschaerts valve gear. Here No 3279 passes Greenwood with the 5.30pm Kings Cross-Newcastle express in 1925. *F R Hebron*

LEFT: In 1938 No 3279 emerged from Doncaster Works rebuilt with two cylinders identical to those fitted to the Class K2 Moguls. No 3279 is seen at Spalding with a Grimsby-Kings Cross express in September 1938. *T G Hepburn*

ABOVE: Robinson GCR Class C4 Atlantic No 6089, in wartime livery, passes Firsby South Junction with a Lincoln-Skegness train on July 27, 1946. There were 27 engines in this class built between 1903-06.
T G Hepburn

RIGHT: One of the four Robinson Class C5 three-cylinder compound 4-4-2s built at Gorton in 1905-06, No 364 *Lady Faringdon,* stands at Nottingham Victoria about 1924. The engine is in the earliest form of L&NER livery and before the addition of 5000 to its number. *T G Hepburn*

ABOVE: Robinson GCR Class C4 Atlantic No 5363 enters Nottingham Victoria with the Sunday 12.15pm Manchester Central-Marylebone express in the mid-1930s. From 1928 the Robinson Atlantics were painted black in company with the small boilered Ivatt Class C2. *T G Hepburn*

BELOW: Raven NER Class C7 three-cylinder Atlantic No 2196 hurries past Croft Spa, south of Darlington, with a Swansea-Newcastle express about 1930. Introduced in 1911 there were 50 engines in this class built during the years up to 1918. *F R Hebron*

L N E R
2196

BELOW: Raven Class C7 Atlantic No 2210 resting on Kings Cross shed before returning north at 12.24am with an excursion train for Wallsend about 1930. Note the NER Class Z painted on the buffer beam of this engine; the former NER works at Darlington and Gateshead did not start using the LNER classifications for NER engines until 1932. *Courtesy Lens of Sutton*

UPPER RIGHT: W Worsdell NER Class C6 4-4-2 No 1794 pilots green-liveried Gresley Class A4 Pacific No 4483 *Kingfisher* on a southbound express from Edinburgh Waverley seen passing St. Margaret's shed on August 1, 1937 Twenty engines of this class were built, ten from Gateshead in 1903-4 as NER Class V, of which No 1794 was the final engine, and ten from Darlington in 1910 as Class V1 with detailed alterations. *L Hanson*

LOWER RIGHT: The down "Queen of Scots" Pullman from Kings Cross to Glasgow accelerates from the Morpeth speed restriction behind Raven Class C7 Atlantic No 2211 about 1930, *F R Hebron*

1794

ABOVE: Reid NBR Class C11 Atlantic No 9904 *Holyrood* passes Haymarket shed with an Edinburgh Waverley-Glasgow Queen Street stopping train in 1927. *F R Hebron*

BELOW: An Aberdeen-London fish train passes Arbroath hauled by Class C11 4-4-2 No 9869 *Bonnie Dundee* in the early 1930s. There were 22 Reid Atlantics, 14 built in 1906, six in 1910 and a final two in 1921. *T G Hepburn*

ABOVE: The morning Carlisle-Edinburgh Waverley train pulls into Hawick behind Reid Class C11 Atlantic No 9879 *Abbotsford* about 1930. *F R Hebron*

BELOW: Class C11 No 9879 *Abbotsford* is seen again running wrong line through Muchalls, north of Stonehaven, in order to pass failed LMS 'Royal Scot' class 4-6-0 No 6108 *Seaforth Highlander,* both with trains for Aberdeen in 1936. *F R Hebron*

ABOVE: The LNER inherited four Pacifics at the Grouping in 1923, two from the GNR and two from the NER. Both designs first appeared in 1922 and it was inevitable that trials between the two types should take place to establish the most suitable for further construction. The pioneer Gresley GNR Class A1 Pacific No 4470 *Great Northern* departs from Kings Cross with the 1.30pm express to Leeds and Bradford in February 1925. *F R Hebron*

BELOW: The second of the two Raven NER Pacifics built in 1922, No 2401 *City of Kingston-upon-Hull,* departs from Edinburgh Waverley with the southbound "Queen of Scots" Pullman in July 1932. Three further Raven Class A2 Pacifics were built at Darlington in 1924. No further engines of this type were built as the Gresley design was chosen for further construction and the A2 Class became extinct in 1937. *T G Hepburn*

ABOVE: The largest express passenger 4-6-0s that came into LNER ownership in 1923 were the six Robinson GCR Lord Faringdon Class B3 four-cylinder engines built at Gorton, one in 1917 and the remainder in 1920. Here No 6165 *Valour,* the Great Central war memorial engine, climbs past New Basford on the northern exit from Nottingham with a Marylebone-Immingham Docks Orient Line boat train in the late 1920s. *T G Hepburn*

BELOW: Class B3 4-6-0 No 6167 departs from Kings Cross with the 11.15 am 'Harrogate Pullman' in 1925. This engine was named *Lloyd George* until 1923, when the nameplates were removed at Kings Cross shed, where they came to light 40 years later when the shed was being demolished! These engines spent five years working on the GN section until the Gresley Pacifics were allowed to work through from Doncaster to Leeds. *F R Hebron*

ABOVE: Robinson GCR 'Immingham' Class B4 4-6-0 No 6101 backs on to empty stock in the sidings outside Skegness in 1925. There were 10 engines in this class, all built in 1906 by Beyer Peacock. *F R Hebron*

BELOW: Robinson GCR 'Sir Sam Fay' Class B2 4-6-0 No 5423 *Sir Sam Fay* pulls forward off the turntable at the north end of Nottingham Victoria on June 6, 1939. The six B2s were built at Gorton in 1912-3. *J P Wilson*

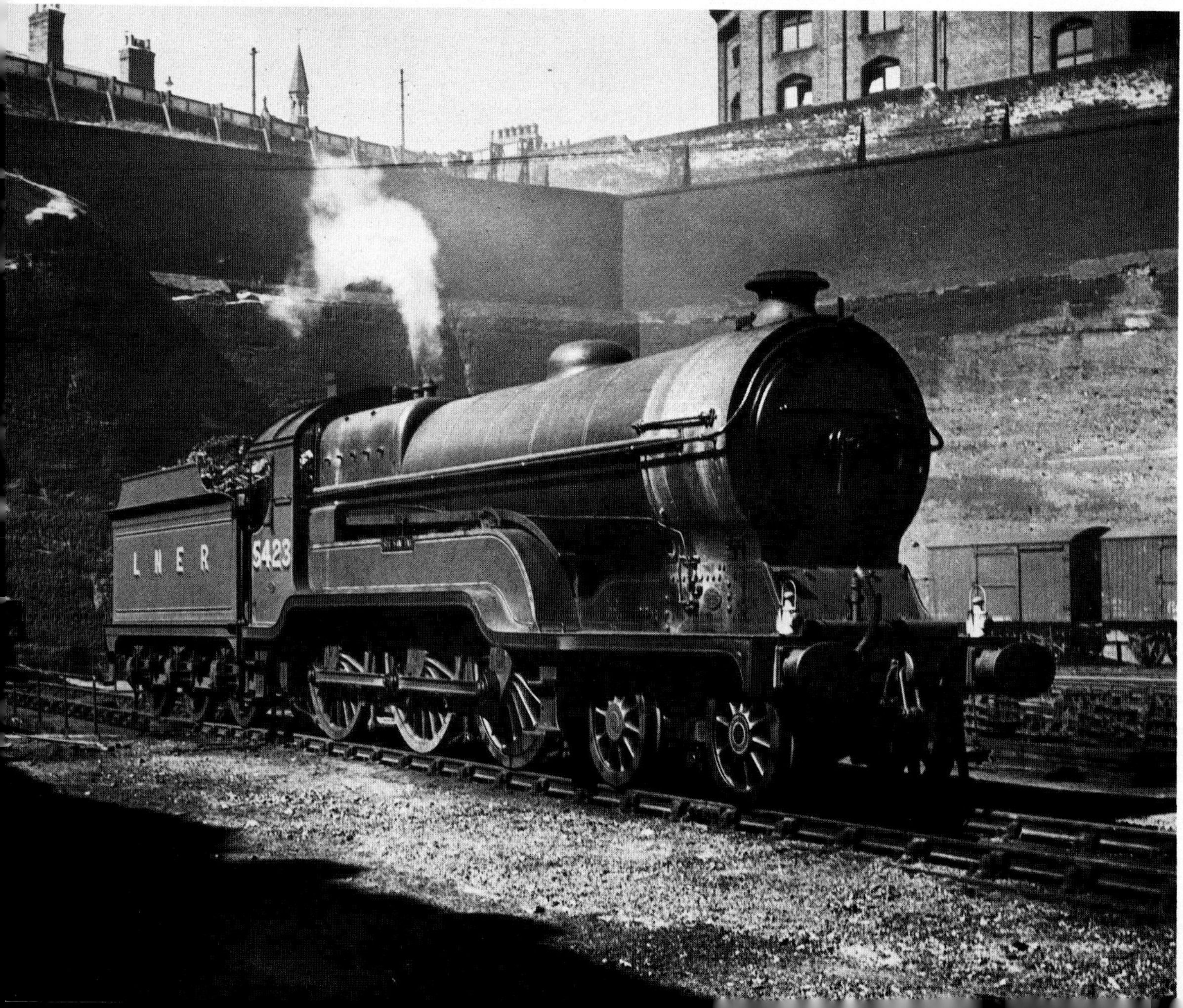

ABOVE: A southbound fish train from Grimsby passes Nottingham Victoria in the late 1920s behind Robinson GCR Class B5 4-6-0 No 5186. The 14 engines in this class, the first Robinson 4-6-0s introduced in 1902, were always known as 'Fish Engines'. *T G Hepburn*

BELOW: Robinson GCR Class B7 four-cylinder 4-6-0 No 5478 is seen at Nottingham Victoria in the 1930s. These mixed-traffic engines first appeared in 1918 and a total of 38 were built. They were the last of the nine classes of 4-6-0 designed by J G Robinson. *T G Hepburn*

RIGHT: Beautifully turned out, S D Holden GER Class B12 4-6-0 No 8552 tops Bethnal Green bank with the down 'Eastern Belle' Pullman excursion train from Liverpool Street to Clacton about 1930. Between 1911 and 1921 71 of these fine engines were built, 51 from Stratford and the remainder from Beardmore's. Only 70 came into LNER stock, as No 1506 was scrapped when only six months old after the Colchester crash of July 1913. *F R Hebron*

BELOW: In 1928 Beyer Peacock built a further 10 B12s to LNER order fitted with Lentz oscillating-cam valve gear. No 8579 is seen at Nottingham Victoria with a Bradford-Marylebone train while running-in from Gorton in the Autumn of 1928. These 10 engines became Class B12/2. *T G Hepburn*

LOWER RIGHT: Following the trial fitting of ACFI feed-water heaters to three B12s in 1927 a further 50 sets were ordered and fitted in 1931-33. With the start of rebuilding the class with larger boilers with round-top fireboxes two sets of ACFI equipment became redundant; they were fitted to two further B12s in 1934, including No 8552, seen again here fitted with the apparatus at Liverpool Street in 1935. So in all 53 sets of ACFI equipment were fitted to 55 engines. *C R L Coles*

8552
L N E R

ABOVE: The rebuilding of the B12s with larger boilers and round-top fireboxes has already been mentioned. In fact 54 were rebuilt to Class B12/3 between 1932 and 1944. Here Class B12/3 4-6-0 No 8518 heads an up express near Brentwood in the late 1930s. *F R Hebron*

LEFT: The only other constituant that contributed some 4-6-0s to LNER stock was the NER, with four classes. Raven Class B15 4-6-0 No 813 is seen departing from York with an excursion for Scarborough formed of LMS stock in the early 1930s. This was one of 20 engines built at Darlington in 1911-13. *H Gordon Tidey, courtesy Real Photographs Co Ltd*

BELOW: Raven Class B16 three-cylinder 4-6-0 No 914 simmers on York shed in June 1925. Introduced in 1919 this successful design numbered 70 engines when the last appeared in 1924. They were all built at Darlington and 24 were subsequently rebuilt by Gresley and Thompson. *F R Hebron*

E R
914

ABOVE: Ivatt GNR Class D2 4-4-0 No 3049 approaches Hadley Wood North Tunnel at Ganwick with a Hitchin-Kings Cross local in 1938. There were 70 engines in this class built between 1898 and 1909. *C R L Coles*

LEFT: Ivatt GNR Class D2 4-4-0 No 4324, with original footplating, pilots Ivatt Class D3 4-4-0 No 4344 at Grantham with a train for Nottingham in the early 1930s. The D3s were built in 1896-99 and all 51 were rebuilt by Gresley in 1912-28. *T G Hepburn*

RIGHT: Ivatt GNR Class D1 4-4-0 No 62N passes Wood Green with a Kings Cross-Hitchin local early in 1925. The 15 D1s, built in 1911, were all transferred to Scotland soon after this picture was taken. The N suffix to the number was used before the LNER decided to add 3000 to the numbers of GNR locomotives.
F R Hebron

BELOW: A Derby-Grantham local hauled by Ivatt Class D2 4-4-0 No 4328 has just passed under the GCR main line before joining it at Bagthorpe Junction with a Derby-Grantham stopping train in the early 1930s.
T G Hepburn

LEFT: Robinson GCR 'Director' Class D10 4-4-0 No 5438 *Worsley Taylor* waits to leave Kings Cross with the very short-lived 'Manchester Pullman' in 1925. The 10 'Directors' were all built at Gorton in 1913. *F R Hebron*

BELOW: Robinson GCR 'Improved Director' Class D11/1 4-4-0 No 5507 *Gerard Powys Dewhurst* climbs Holloway bank out of Kings Cross with the 'Edinburgh Pullman' in 1927. Eleven of these engines were built in 1919-22. *F R Hebron*

ABOVE: The 2.20pm Manchester London Road-Marylebone express leaves Guide Bridge for the climb over Woodhead behind Class D11/1 4-4-0 No 5505 *Ypres. R D Pollard, courtesy N Fields*

RIGHT: A further 24 D11s were ordered in 1924 by the LNER for use in Scotland. Here extremely grimy Class D11/2 4-4-0 No 6388 *Captain Craigengelt* passes Lochmuir summit with an Edinburgh Waverley-Dundee train in the early 1930s. *T G Hepburn*

ABOVE: Pollitt GCR (MS&LR) Class D6 4-4-0 No 5880 at Immingham shed on May 11, 1938. This class was introduced in 1897 and 33 were built in the three years up to 1899 for use on the newly-completed London extension. *J G Dewing*

BELOW: Parker GCR (MS&LR) Class D7 4-4-0 No 5562 runs light into Cleethorpes in the late 1920s. Built in 1887-92, there were 31 engines in this class. Note the 'flower pot' chimney fitted to the two engines on this page — a feature that spoilt the looks of so many GCR engines in LNER days. *T G Hepburn*

ABOVE: A Lincoln-Cleethorpes stopping train formed of vintage six-wheeled stock approaches Littlefield Lane level crossing, Grimsby, hauled by Robinson Class D9 4-4-0 No 5109 about 1930. Between 1901 and 1904 a total of 40 D9s were built. *F R Hebron*

BELOW: J Holden GER Class D13 4-4-0 No 8036 passes Exton Road Sidings as it approaches Kings Lynn with a train from Hunstanton about 1930. The 60 engines in this class, 58 of which came into LNER ownership, were rebuilt in 1905-08 from 2-4-0s built in 1886-97. *F R Hebron*

ABOVE: J Holden GER 'Claud Hamilton' Class D14 4-4-0 No 8879 approaches Romford in June 1926 with a Liverpool Street-Southend Victoria stopping train. The 'Claud Hamilton' class was introduced in 1900 and 41 engines were built to this design before Belpaire fireboxes were introduced; 70 further engines, LNER Class D15, were built up to 1911 and all the earlier examples were rebuilt with Belpaire fireboxes by 1931. *F R Hebron*

BELOW: In 1923 10 further engines were built to the design of A J Hill and known as 'Super Clauds'. Here Class D16 4-4-0 No 8783 makes a smoky ascent of Brentwood bank with the down 'Eastern Belle' Pullman bound for Clacton in 1927. It is hard to believe that this scruffy 'Super Claud', probably a last minute substitute for the booked engine on this star turn, was to become one of those two shining Royal 'Clauds' kept at Cambridge. *F R Hebron*

LEFT: In 1926 a start was made in fitting all the 'Claud Hamilton' 4-4-0s with extended smokeboxes. Here one of the original 10 engines built in 1900, No 8895 rebuilt to Class D15/2 and with a tender used when the engines were oil fired, passes March on June 18, 1936. *J G Dewing*

BELOW: Class D16/2 4-4-0 No 8787, one of the 10 'Super Clauds' heads a down Clacton train near Brentwood about 1930. This was the other Cambridge Royal 'Claud' that retained green livery and a copper-capped chimney. In addition to the original 10 'Super Clauds' a further 30 D15 engines were rebuilt to this class. Then in 1933 rebuilding to Class D16/3 with round-top fireboxes commenced. *F R Hebron*

RIGHT: M Stirling H&BR Class D24 4-4-0 No 2429 stands inside Hull Springhead shops while in store on February 10, 1934 shortly before being withdrawn. There were five of these 4-4-0s built by Kitson & Co in 1910 and fitted with domed boilers by the LNER from 1929. *T E Rounthwaite*

BELOW: W Worsdell NER Class D17/2 4-4-0 No 1906 hurries down the East Coast main line between Stannington and Plessey with the 1.38pm Newcastle-Alnwick local in March 1939. There were 30 engines in Class D17/2, being the former NER Class Q, which were built in 1896-97; Class D17/1 comprised the 20 NER Class M engines built in 1892-94 *E E Smith*

2021
N E R
2021

ABOVE: W Worsdell NER Class D20 4-4-0 No 2021 accelerates away from York with a Leeds train about 1926. The leading four vans are LMS (ex-LNWR) stock. This was one of Wilson Worsdell's very successful Class R 4-4-0s introduced in 1899 and multiplied to 60 engines by 1907. *H Gordon Tidey, Courtesy Real Photographs Co. Ltd*

RIGHT: The Class R was followed by Worsdell's Class R1, the last 4-4-0s built for the NER. Here, as LNER Class D21, No 1237 leaves York with a Leeds train about 1926. Only 10 of these engines were built, in 1908-09. *H Gordon Tidey, courtesy Real Photographs Co. Ltd*

ABOVE: Reid NBR 'Scott' Class D30/1 4-4-0 No 9363 *Hal o'the Wynd* leaves Edinburgh Waverley with a Thornton Junction train on August 4, 1938. This was one of the first two superheated 'Scotts' built in 1912 followed by a further 25 modified engines in 1914-20. *L Hanson*

LEFT: Holmes NBR Class D31 4-4-0 No 9574 leaves Perth with a Ladybank train in the early 1930s. No 9574 was the first engine of its class built in 1884 and was rebuilt by Reid in 1911. *T G Hepburn*

ABOVE: Another Class D31 4-4-0, No 9642, enters North Queensferry as it leaves the Forth Bridge with a down local on August 25, 1936. In all there were 48 D31s, built in 1884-99. *E R Wethersett, Ian Allan Library*

BELOW: Manson GNSR Class D43 4-4-0 No 6813, still fitted with smokebox wingplates, leaves Aberdeen with a Ballater train about 1928. There were only three engines in this class, built in 1890. *Locomotive Publishing Co, Ian Allan Library*

78

L N E R
10249
THING
CKYARD.

UPPER LEFT: J Holden GER Class E4 2-4-0 No 7478 leaves Penrith with a Darlington train in the late 1930s. This was one of six E4s sent to the NE Area in 1935 and later fitted with side-window cabs for working over Stainmore. *Eric Treacy*

LOWER LEFT: Wheatley NBR Class E7 2-4-0 No 10249 at Inverkeithing about 1925 with a local for Dunfermline. Six of these engines built in 1873 came into LNER stock. *T G Heburn*

ABOVE: A post-war view of Class E4 2-4-0 No 2783 (pre-1946 No 7477) leaving Audley End with the branch train for Bartlow on March 27, 1948. There were 100 engines in this class, built in 1891-1902. *E R Wethersett, Ian Allan Library*

RIGHT: Only one class of 4-2-2 tender engines came into LNER stock. They were the six Pollitt GCR Class X4 engines built in 1900. Here Class X4 4-2-2 No 5972 takes part in the Stockton & Darlington Centenary procession on July 2, 1925. *F R Hebron*

ABOVE: Ivatt GNR Class J4 0-6-0 No 4138 heads a packed Hatfield-Southend excursion train formed of GNR four-wheeled coaches near Romford on July 1, 1926. This engine was built in 1900 to a design introduced by Patrick Stirling in1873 and was rebuilt to Class J3 in 1927. *F R Hebron*

BELOW: T W Worsdell NER Class J21 0-6-0 No 30 stands outside Darlington shed on July 15, 1936. This engine was built at Gateshead in 1890 as a two-cylinder Worsdell-von Borries compound. There were 201 engines in the class built in 1886-95, of which 171 were compounds, later converted to simples in 1901-13. *J G Dewing*

ABOVE: GNR Class J6 0-6-0 No 3602 climbs past Ganwick with the 5.54pm Kings Cross-Dunstable train on August 3, 1938. This was a regular turn for one of these engines designed by Ivatt and built in 1911-22. A total of 110 were built, the first 15 to Ivatt's design and the remainder, including No 3602, to a modified design by Gresley, who became CME of the GNR in 1911. *E R Wethersett, Ian Allan Library*

BELOW: An up goods train heads south from Plessey behind W Worsdell NER Class J27 0-6-0 No 2340 on September 28, 1938. The first J27 was built in 1906 and 80 were built up to 1909, then in 1921-23 a further 35, including No 2340, were built with superheaters and piston valves. *E E Smith*

LEFT: Robinson GCR Class J11 0-6-0 No 5223 runs into Romiley with a Manchester London Road-Hayfield train on April 10, 1939. Introduced in 1901 a total of 174 engines were built to this design up to 1910. *R D Pollard, courtesy N Fields*

BELOW: A long goods train leaves Kings Lynn hauled by T W Worsdell GER Class J15 0-6-0 No 7869 about 1930. This class originally numbered 289 engines, built in 1883-1913, but 17 had been withdrawn before the grouping, so the LNER took 272 into its stock in 1923. *F R Hebron*

ABOVE: Hill GER Class J19/1 0-6-0 No 8250 passes through Spalding with a goods train bound for March about 1936. There were 25 of these engines built in 1916-20 and they were fitted with new boilers with round-top fireboxes in 1934-39, becoming Class J19/2. At the same time the 10 Class J18 engines built 1912-13 were rebuilt to Class J19/2, three becoming J19/1 engines at first. *T G Hepburn*

RIGHT: Reid NBR Class J37 0-6-0 No 9273 is caught by the evening sun as it approaches the Dalmeny end of the Forth Bridge with a southbound goods train in 1936. This was the final class of NBR 0-6-0 which totalled 104 engines, built in 1914-21. *F R Hebron*

ABOVE: Hill GER Class J20 0-6-0 No 8278 heads a Whitemoor-Temple Mills coal train in the short gap between Littlebury and Audley End tunnels on August 20, 1935. The 25 engines in this class built in 1920-22 were the most powerful 0-6-0s in the country until the advent of the Bulleid Q1s of the Southern Railway in 1942. *E R Wethersett, Ian Allan Library*

LEFT: Gresley GNR Class K2 2-6-0 No 4681 approaches Sandy with an up express goods on May 1, 1937. This was Gresley's second 2-6-0 design for the GNR and 65 were built in 1913-21. The original 10 K1 engines built in 1912-13 were rebuilt to Class K2 in 1931-37. *L Hanson*

L N E R
2264
2264

UPPER LEFT: Raven NER Class Q6 0-8-0 No 3420 (pre-1946 No 2263) passes Heaton & Byker with an up goods about 1948. Between 1913 and 1921 a total of 120 engines of this class were built. *E E Smith*

LOWER LEFT: An eastbound goods passes through Goole behind Class Q6 No 2264 in the late 1930s. *Courtesy Lens of Sutton*

ABOVE: Robinson GCR Class Q4 0-8-0 No 6075 pounds past Godley East Junction with an up empty wagon train on August 12, 1933. In 1902-11 89 of these 0-8-0s were built and 13, including No 6075, were rebuilt as 0-8-0Ts in 1942-45. *R D Pollard, courtesy N Fields*

RIGHT: Ivatt GNR Class Q1 0-8-0 No 3427 at Kings Cross shed in 1926. There were 55 Ivatt 0-8-0s built in 1901-09. This engine carries the GNR Class K1 painted on its buffer bream, probably as a result of repairs at an NER works. *F R Hebron*

ABOVE: Gresley GNR Class O1 2-8-0 No 3475 brings an up goods train round the curve from Brookman's Park towards Potters Bar in the autumn of 1938. This was Gresley's first 2-8-0 design and 20 were built in 1913-19. One additional engine was built in 1918, Class O2 No 3461, which was the first Gresley engine to have three cylinders.
E E Smith

BELOW: An un-identified Robinson GCR Class O4 2-8-0 heads a down goods past Bagthorpe Junction on July 2, 1932. Introduced in 1911, there were originally 126 of these fine engines, built for the GCR up to 1914, plus a further 19 with large boilers of 1918-21 that become LNER Class O5. A further 521 were built to Ministry of Munitions order in 1917-19 for use by the ROD during World War I. Three of these came into GCR stock in 1919, while the LNER bought 273 during the years 1923-29.
T G Hepburn

N E
9658

ABOVE: Class N7/1 0-6-2T No 9658 (pre-1946 No 935) leaves Loughton with an Epping train in 1947. The conductor rails are laid for the extension of the LT Central Line to Epping. A J Hill's GER Class N7 0-6-2T was introduced in 1915, but only 12 engines were built up to 1921, with 10 more coming out in 1923-24. The design was then chosen by Gresley for further construction and in 1925-28 112 were built. *J G Dewing*

RIGHT: Gresley Class N2/4 0-6-2T No 9586 (pre-1946 No 2680) leaves Hadley Wood South tunnel with a Moorgate-Hatfield train in 1947. This GNR design was also chosen for further construction and in addition to the 60 engines built in 1920-21 47 more were constructioned in 1925-29. *F R Hebron*

ABOVE: Robinson GCR Class A5 4-6-2T No 5024 barks its way up the bank from Rickmansworth at Chorley Wood with the 3.25pm Marylebone-Brackley train in June 1938. Introduced in 1911, a total of 31 of these Pacific tanks were built to GCR order.
E R Wethersett, Ian Allan Library

UPPER RIGHT: Class A5 4-6-2T No 5129 at Ganwick with the 5.10pm Kings Cross-Hatfield train in 1929. A number of A5s found themselve working in the GN Kings Cross area at various dates between 1928 and 1940. No 5129, as BR 69814, was back at Kings Cross briefly in 1960. *F R Hebron*

LOWER RIGHT: In 1925-26 a further batch of 13 A5s were built by Hawthorn, Leslie & Co to LNER order for service in the North Eastern area. Here No 1767 of this batch waits to leave Darlington Bank Top Station with a Saltburn train about 1930. *Locomotive Publishing Co, Ian Allan Library*

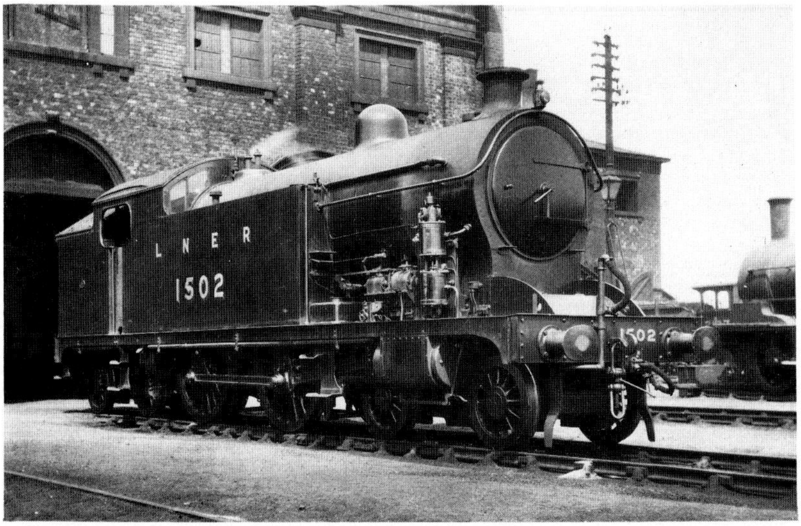

LEFT: Raven NER Class H1 4-4-4T No 1502 is seen outside Darlington shed about 1934. The 45 Class H1 engines built in 1913-22 were the only 4-4-4Ts inherited by the LNER in 1923 and they were later rebuilt as 4-6-2Ts of Class A8. Just one year after the last was converted the LNER found itself with eight more 4-4-4Ts taken over from London Transport in 1937. *Courtesy Lens of Sutton*

RIGHT: One of the rebuilt Class H1 engines as Class A8 4-6-2T No 9871 (pre-1946 No 1518) is seen at West Hartlepool shed in the Summer of 1949. The rebuilding of these engines took place at Darlington between 1931 and 1936. *E E Smith*

LEFT: One of the 10 W Worsdell NER Class A6 4-6-2Ts built in 1907-08, No 695 is seen at Whitby in the mid 1930s. These tanks were originally constructed as 4-6-0Ts for working over the hilly coast line between Whitby and Scarborough and were rebuilt as 4-6-2Ts in 1914-17. *T G Hepburn*

ABOVE: W Worsdell NER Class N10 0-6-2T No 1716 heads a short coal train on the Tanfield mineral line near Marley Hill in 1937. Class N10 comprised 20 engines built in 1902-03. *E E Smith*

BELOW: An Esk Valley line train for Stockton passes Bog Hall Junction as it leaves Whitby behind W Worsdell NER Class G5 0-4-4T No 7308 (pre-1946 No 1775) on June 5, 1947. All 110 engines of this class were built at Darlington in 1894-1901. *J P Wilson*

L N E R
5179

N E
7375

UPPER LEFT: Robinson GCR Class C13 4-4-2T No 5179 approaches New Mills with a Manchester-Hayfield train on September 4, 1938. A total of 40 of these Atlantic tanks were built in 1903-05. *R D Pollard, courtesy N Fields*

LOWER LEFT: The branch train from Saffron Walden arrives at Audley End behind Ivatt GNR Class C12 4-4-2T No 7375 (pre-1946 No 4520) on March 27, 1948. This class totalled 60 engines built at Doncaster in 1898-1907. *E R Wethersett, Ian Allan Library*

RIGHT: T W Worsdell GER Class F4 2-4-2T No 7072 departs from Liverpool Street with a Chingford train in the 1930s. A total of 160 Gobblers were built between 1884 and 1909. Only 118 came into LNER stock as F4s while 32 had been rebuilt to Class F5, two being erroneously classified F6. *Ian Allan Library*

BELOW: Johnson GNSR Class G10 0-4-4T No 6885 heads out of Aberdeen with a Banchory train about 1928. The nine engines of this class were built by Neilson & Co in 1909. *Locomotive Publishing Co, Ian Allan Library*

ABOVE: Hill GER Class Y4 0-4-0T No 8126 (pre-1946 No 7228) pauses during shunting at Stratford on September 6, 1947. Five of these powerful little engines were built in 1913-20. *J G Dewing*

BELOW: One of the two T W Worsdell NER Class J78 0-6-0 crane tanks built at Gateshead in 1888, No 590 slumbers at the back of York shed where it acted as shed pilot. *Courtesy Lens of Sutton*

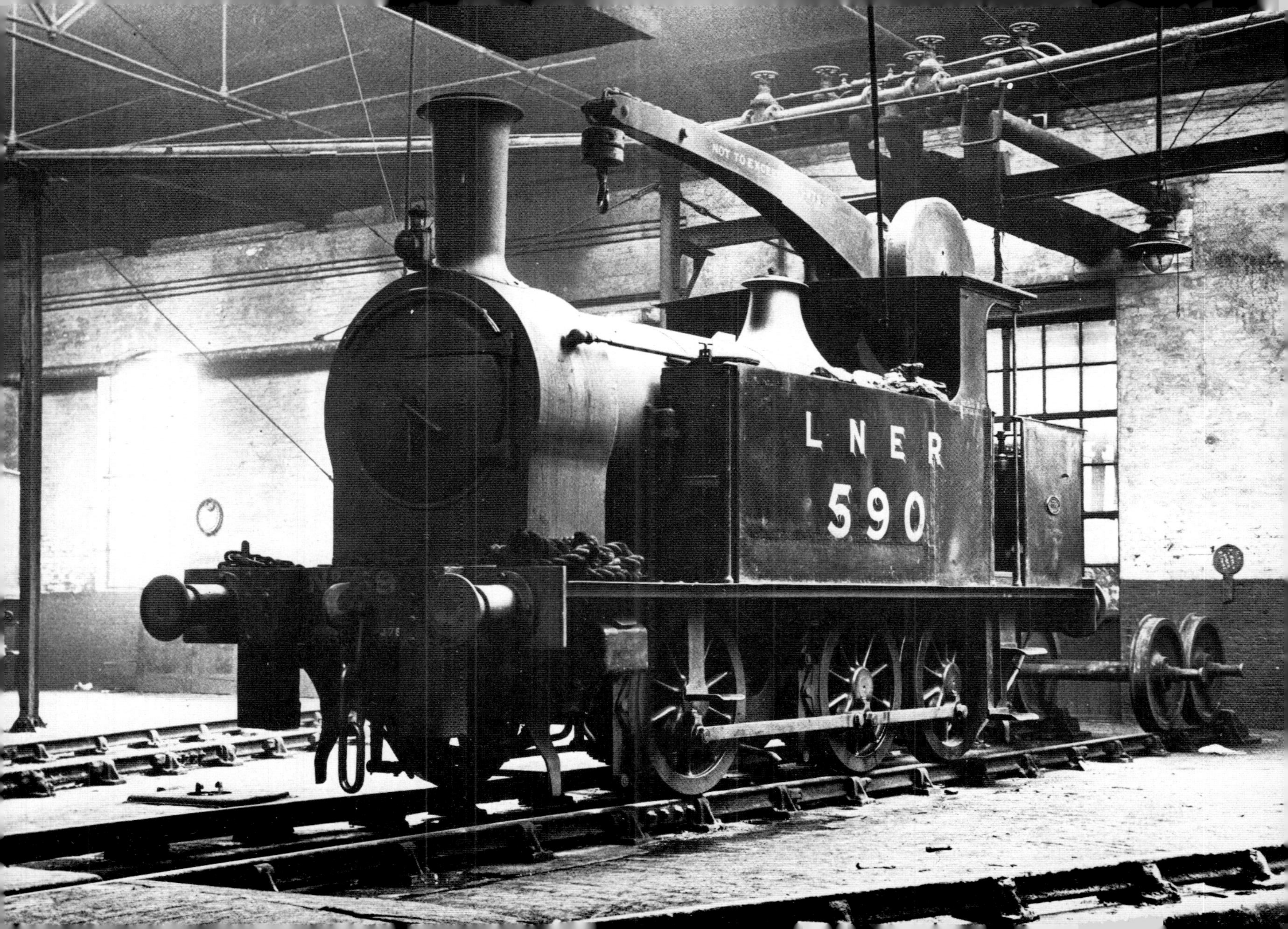
LNER
590

ABOVE: Ivatt GNR Class J52 0-6-0ST No 4224 at New England shed on May 21, 1938. In 1897-1909 a total of 85 of these saddle-tanks were built. They were the final development of the Stirling 0-6-0ST first introduced in 1874. *J G Dewing*

BELOW: Holmes NBR Class J83 0-6-0T No 8474 (pre-1946 No 9827) rests between station pilot duties at the east end of Edinburgh Waverley on July 28, 1946. There were 40 engines in this class built in 1900-01. *E R Wethersett, Ian Allan Library*

RIGHT: Pollitt GCR (MS&LR) Class J62 0-6-0ST No 5890 at Immingham on May 15, 1938. A dozen of these engines were built at Gorton in 1897 primarily for working in Grimsby Docks, but they later saw service at Immingham and Birkenhead, amongst other places. *J G Dewing*

LEFT: Reid NBR Class J88 0-6-0T No 9836 at St Margaret's shed, Edinburgh on August 1, 1937. This was the first of 35 of these tanks built at Cowlairs in 1904-12. *L Hanson*

RIGHT: The first GNR Class J50 0-6-0T No 3221 built in 1922 is seen at Peterborough in 1927. Ten of these engines were built in 1922 followed by a further 62 in 1924-39. Also 30 earlier engines built in 1914-19 to Class J51 were rebuilt to Class J50 in 1929-35. *F R Hebron*

ABOVE: In 1923 a further 10 Gresley Class A1 Pacifics ordered by the GNR were turned out from Doncaster works. The first of these engines was No 1472, later 4472 *Flying Scotsman* seen here at Kings Cross early in 1925. The engine is in the special finish for the British Empire Exhibition at Wembley with the LNER coat of arms on the cabside. *F R Hebron*

BELOW: Another of the 1923-built Class A1 Pacifics, No 4479 *Robert the Devil,* is seen in the engine yard at Kings Cross in 1925. In these two pictures both engines still have short travel valve gear, the large GNR chimney and high cab roof. A further 40 A1s were ordered in 1923. *F R Hebron*

ABOVE: The 40 Gresley Class A1 Pacifics ordered late in 1923 entered service between June 1924 and July 1925 with Nos 2543-62 coming from Doncaster works and Nos 2563-82 from the North British Locomotive Co Ltd. Here Doncaster-built No 2558 *Tracery* departs from Grantham with a Kings Cross-Leeds Central express in the early 1930s. These engines were built with short-travel valve gear and were given long-travel gear in 1927-31. *T G Hepburn*

UPPER RIGHT: One of the North British-built Class A1 Pacifics, No 2575 *Galopin* takes water from Langley water troughs with the up "Flying Scotsman" about 1930. Engines Nos 2568-82 were equipped with Westinghouse brake pumps for working in the North Eastern Area, the pump being clearly visible in the photograph. Note also the 'Class 4.6.2' painted on the buffer beam of both engines illustrated on this page. *F R Hebron*

LOWER RIGHT: Commencing in July 1927 a start was made in reboilering the Class A1 Pacifics with new 220lb sq/in boilers in place of the original 180lb sq/in boilers. Five engines were done in 1927-28, but it was not until the war years that conversion began in earnest as the original boilers wore out and they were all done by the end of 1948. The re-boilered engines became Class A3 and No 2578 *Bayardo,* converted in 1928, lays a heavy smoke screen over Potters Bar with the 5.30pm Kings Cross-Newcastle express about 1930. *F R Hebron*

Nº 2575

L N E R

RIGHT: The first engine converted to Class A3 in 1927 was No 4480 *Enterprise,* seen here about to plunge into Potters Bar Tunnel with the 4pm Kings Cross-Newcastle express on August 12, 1938. Arrival at Newcastle was at 10.7 pm, 2 hours 10 minutes after the "Coronation" express for Edinburgh which also left Kings Cross at 4 pm. *E R Wethersett, Ian Allan Library*

BELOW: In 1928-35 a further series of 27 Gresley Pacifics were built at Doncaster to Class A3. Here Class A3 Pacific No 2501 *Colombo,* built in 1934, passes Barkston with the 8.55 am Glasgow Queen Street-Kings Cross express on August 2, 1937. This train reached Kings Cross at 5.35 pm. *T G Hepburn*

No 2501
254

Gresley Class A1 Pacific No 4476 *Royal Lancer* climbs from Grantham to Stoke summit with the up non-stop "Flying Scotsman" on a stormy day in 1928. The non-stop service began on May 1, 1928 and ran each summer up to the outbreak of war then again in 1948-61. Ten corridor tenders were built to enable the engine crews to be changed over halfway. These were attached to the Pacifics most likely to be used on this duty and were changed from time to time. No 4476 held the record for having a corridor tender from April 1928 until July 1937, by which time Gresley A4 Pacifics had taken over the non-stop working and the corridor tenders.
T G Hepburn

FLYING SCOTSMAN
4476
4476

ABOVE: Two Class A3 Pacifics were the subject of smoke deflection experiments in the early 1930s. Here No 2747 *Coronach,* with the upper part of its smokebox partitioned off to act as an air duct, climbs away from Grantham with an up express in 1932. *T G Hepburn*

BELOW: The other A3 was No 2751 *Humorist,* which, after being used for a series of smoke deflection experiments, was fitted with a Kylchap double blastpipe and chimney in 1937. It is seen in this condition leaving Grantham with a Kings Cross-Leeds express in 1937. This remained the sole A3 with a double chimney until BR fitted to them to all the class from 1958. *T G Hepburn*

ABOVE: In 1920-21 Gresley built 10 Class K3 2-6-0s for the GNR. Subsequent to the grouping the design was chosen as a group standard class and a further 183 were built between 1924 and 1937. Here No 125 leaves New Southgate with the 3 pm Kings Cross-Peterborough all-stations train during the general strike in May 1926. The locomotive was being manned by volunteers. This engine was from the first batch of 50 K3s built by the LNER at Darlington. Note the NER style cab and the 'Class 2.6..0' painted on its buffer beam. *F R Hebron*

BELOW: One of the later Class K3 Moguls, No 2766 passes Retford with a up excursion train in the early 1930s. *F R Hebron*

ABOVE: Gresley Class K3 Mogul No 186, one of the engines built at Darlington in 1925 and here fitted with a standard cab but unusually coupled with a GNR tender, cautiously passes through Grantham in 1932 with a down cattle train. *T G Hepburn*

BELOW: The first new class introduced by the LNER were the two Gresley Class P1 2-8-2s built in 1925. Here Class P1 Mikado No 2394, shorn of booster engine, passes Potters Bar with a New England-Hornsey coal train on June 18, 1937. *A C Cawston*

ABOVE: In 1925 there also appeared the solitary Gresley Class U1 2-8-0+0-8-2 Beyer-Garratt engine No 2395 designed for banking duties on the Worsborough incline and built by Beyer, Peacock & Co Ltd. No 2395 is seen taking part in the Stockton & Darlington Railway Centenary procession on July 2, 1925. It was the most powerful steam locomotive ever to run in this country and was basically a pair of Class O2 three-cylinder 2-8-0s under one boiler.
F R Hebron

BELOW: Gresley Class J38 0-6-0 No 1440 heads an eastbound freight train at Gorgie, Edinburgh in July 1926. The 35 engines of this class were designed and built at Darlington in 1926 for heavy mineral service in the Fife and Lothian coal fields of Scotland.
T G Hepburn

UPPER RIGHT: Following the Class J38 0-6-0s Darlington produced the first of the Class J39 0-6-0s with driving wheels 5ft 2in in diameter — six inches larger than the J38s. Batches of these engines were built every year from 1926 to 1938 and a final batch in 1941, by which time the class totalled 289. Here Class J39 0-6-0 No 2964 clatters down the Great Eastern main line at Chadwell Heath with a goods train on May 30, 1933. *E R Wethersett, Ian Allan Library*

LOWER RIGHT: In 1932 the first of a series of 41 Gresley Class O2 three-cylinder 2-8-0s came into service. No 2956, built in 1932, passes Trumpington with a Temple Mills-Whitemoor goods on April 16, 1938. The LNER already had 26 O2s built to GNR order in 1918-24. *E R Wethersett, Ian Allan Library*

No 2964

RIGHT: Gresley 'Shire' Class D49/1 three-cylinder 4-4-0 No 2760 *Westmorland* departs from Edinburgh Waverley with a stopping train for Glasgow Queen Street in the early 1930s. This was the last engine of Class D49 built with piston valves; all later engines having poppet valves. The class was designed and built at Darlington using the same boiler as the Class J39 0-6-0 and made its first appearance towards the end of 1927.
T G Hepburn

BELOW: One of the earlier 'Shire' Class D49/1 engines, No 250 *Perthshire* fitted with Westinghouse brake pump, poses with its crew on Perth shed about 1930. The engine carries the "Flying Scotsman" headboard for the photograph, but these engines did carry the headboard when working the Perth portion to Edinburgh. Ultimately there were 34 'Shire' and 42 'Hunt' Class D49/2 engines with Lentz rotary-cam poppet valve gear. Six 'Shires' had been built as Class D49/3 with Lentz oscillating-cam valve gear but these were rebuilt to Class D49/1.
T G Hepburn

FLYING
SCOTSMAN
L N E R
250
250

L N E R
310

INVERNESS-SHIRE
329
L N E R
E R

UPPER LEFT: Class D49/1 4-4-0 No 310 *Kinross-shire* at Falkland Road with an up fish train from Dundee in the early 1930s. *T G Hepburn*

LOWER LEFT: Class D49/3 4-4-0 No 329 *Inverness-shire* on the Grantham turntable in the 1930s. The six of this class with oscillating-cam poppet valve gear were rebuilt to Class D49/1 in 1938. *T G Hepburn*

ABOVE: 'Hunt' Class D49/2 4-4-0 No 298 *The Pytchley* departs from Hull with inspection saloons in the mid-1930s. *Courtesy Lens of Sutton*

RIGHT: The 12.56 pm Newcastle - Southampton approaches Northallerton behind Class D49/2 4-4-0 No 357 *The Fernie* on July 21, 1938. *J P Wilson.*

ABOVE: Gresley Class B17 three-cylinder 4-6-0 No 2848 *Arsenal* waits to leave Sheffield Victoria with the 9.30am Newcastle-Swansea train on August 29, 1936. Class B17 made its appearance in 1928 designed for use on the restricted GE section, but in pre-war days they ranged over a much wider area. *J P Wilson*

LEFT: A fish train from Hull approaches Hessle behind brand-new Class B17 4-6-0 No 2837 *Thorpe Hall* on March 11, 1933. Nos 2800-47 had the short wheelbase GE-type tenders when built. *Lance Brown*

RIGHT: In 1937 two B17s were fitted with streamlined casings for working the "East Anglian" express. Here No 2859 *East Anglian* approaches Chadwell Heath with the up "East Anglian", the 12 noon Norwich-Liverpool Street arriving at 2.10 pm. *E R Wethersett, Ian Allan Library*

BELOW: Class B17 No 2818 *Wynyard Park* storms past Whittlesford with the 3.56pm Cambridge - Liverpool Street on July 30, 1934. A total of 73 B17s were built in 1928-37. *E R Wethersett, Ian Allan Library*

FLYING SCOTSMAN
№ 10000

№ 10000
LNER

UPPER LEFT: The experimental Gresley Class W1 high-pressure four-cylinder compound 4-6-4 No 10000 departs from Kings Cross on its first run with the non-stop "Flying Scotsman" for Edinburgh on August 1, 1930. It had worked the up train the previous day. No 10000 was built in 1929 at Darlington fitted with a Yarrow 450lb sq/in water tube boiler. On the next line stands Class A1 Pacific No 2582 *Sir Hugo* at the head of the 10.5 am "Junior Scotsman". *Fox Photos*

LOWER LEFT: No 10000 with its water-tube boiler proved a troublesome engine to maintain and after several years disuse was rebuilt as a conventional Gresley three-cylinder engine in the style of the Class A4 Pacifics, but retaining the unique Baltic wheel arrangement. Here the rebuilt Class W1 4-6-4 No 10000 emerges from Potters Bar Tunnel with the 4pm Kings Cross-Newcastle express about 1938. *Eric Treacy*

ABOVE: In 1934 Doncaster built the first two Gresley Class P2 three-cylinder 2-8-2s for service on the Aberdeen-Edinburgh route. Seen here is the first, No 2001 *Cock o'the North,* showing the Kylchap double blastpipe and chimney. It was also fitted with an ACFI feed water heater and Lentz rotary-cam poppet valve gear. The second engine, No 2002 *Earl Marischal,* had the conventional Gresley conjugated valve gear, Kylchap blastpipe but no feed water heater. *Ian Allan Library*

OVERLEAF: Class P2 Mikado No 2001 *Cock o'the North* is prepared at Kings Cross prior to a demonstration run in 1934. Class N2 0-6-2T No 4612 stands on the adjacent track. *F R Hebron*

COCK O' THE NORTH

2001
L N E

Nº 2003
CAMP
COFFEE

ABOVE: The introduction of the Gresley 4-6-4 and 2-8-2s had perhaps prepared the railway-minded public for things to come, but the initial appearance of the first Gresley Class A4 Pacific No 2509 *Silver Link* in September 1935 created a sensation. It was not just the streamlined shape but the silver-grey livery of the engine and "Silver Jubilee" train it was to haul that attracted great interest. Here *Silver Link* is seen overtaking one of the pioneer Gresley GNR Class K3 Moguls, No 4008, at New Southgate with the 5.45pm Kings Cross-Newcastle express one Saturday evening before the famous trial run with the "Silver Jubilee" train on September 27, 1935 when it averaged 100mph for 43 miles on end. Four A4s were built at Doncaster in 1935 for working the "Silver Jubilee" express between Kings Cross and Newcastle in 4 hours exactly at an average speed of 67.08 mph. *F R Hebron*

UPPER LEFT: In 1936 four further Class P2 Mikados were built. These had the same wedge-shaped front end as the A4 Pacifics, as this had proved particularly effective in lifting the exhaust clear of the cab. No 2005 *Thane of Fife* is seen climbing away from Inverkeithing with the 1.9pm Edinburgh Waverley-Dundee train on August 28, 1936. *E R Wethersett, Ian Allan Library*

LOWER LEFT: Class P2 No 2003 *Lord President* rolls into Kirkcaldy with the 9 am Aberdeen-Edinburgh Waverley express on August 26, 1936. The two earlier P2s were altered to conform with these later engines, but in 1943-44 the whole class were rebuilt as Pacifics by Edward Thompson. *E R Wethersett, Ian Allan Library*

Nº 4488

ABOVE: Further construction of Class A4 Pacifics expanded the class to 35 examples in 1936-38. Nine engines of this series were painted in the standard LNER apple green, but all the remainder came out in garter blue livery to match the streamlined coaches of the "Coronation" and "West Riding Limited" expresses introduced in 1937. The first of the garter blue A4s, No 4488 *Union of South Africa,* passes through Princes Street Gardens on August 4, 1938 with the 6.40 am Aberdeen-Edinburgh Waverley express conveying through coaches for Kings Cross taken forward in the "Flying Scotsman". *L Hanson*

RIGHT: Class A4 Pacific No 4492 *Dominion of New Zealand* about to depart from Kings Cross with the 10 am non-stop "Flying Scotsman" on July 22, 1937. This engine was in the process of putting in ten consecutive turns on the "Flying Scotsman" between July 18 and 27. It then had two days as standby for the "Coronation" and then resumed the non-stop working to Edinburgh for no less than 44 days, including the Sunday turns with ordinary expresses. *J P Wilson*

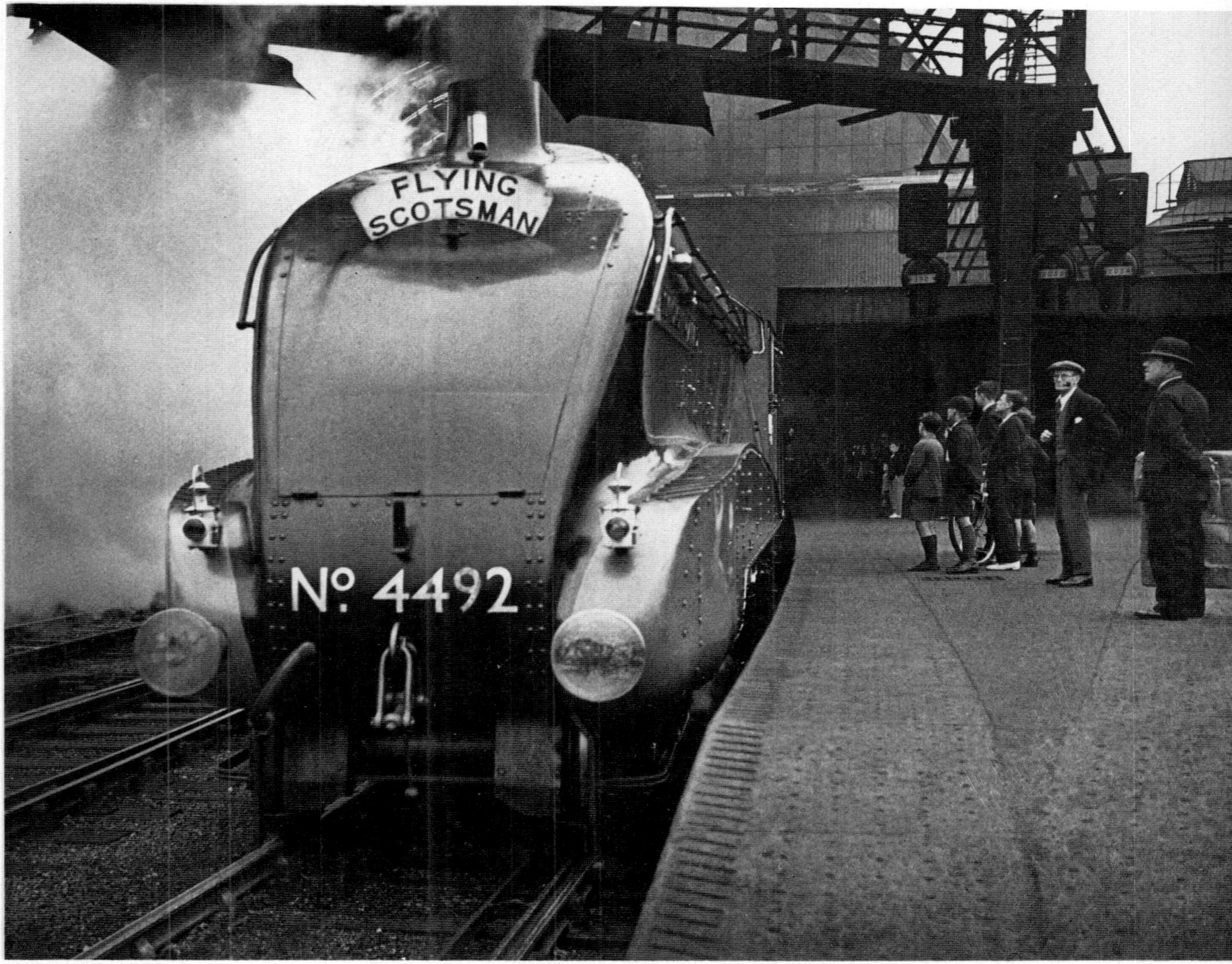

LEFT: Apple-green Class A4 Pacific No 4484 *Falcon* arrives at Kings Cross with the up "Flying Scotsman" in 1937. These and the silver-grey A4s were all painted garter blue in 1937-38.
C R L Coles

BELOW: No 4492 *Dominion of New Zealand,* now fitted with an NZGR chime whistle, hurtles through Grantham with the down "Coronation" from Kings Cross to Edinburgh on July 4, 1939. *T G Hepburn*

ABOVE: The up "Silver Jubilee" passes through York behind No 4902 *Seagull* on July 19, 1938. This was one of the four A4s built with Kylchap double blastpipes. *J P Wilson*

BELOW: The down "Flying Scotsman" waits to leave Newcastle Central with No 12 *Commonwealth of Australia* (pre-1946 No 4491) in 1947. Note the side skirting removed in 1941-42. *Kenneth Oldham*

ABOVE: Gresley Class V1 2-6-2T No 2920 passes Dalmeny Junction with the 4.33 pm Edinburgh Waverley-Stirling train on August 21, 1937. *E R Wethersett, Ian Allan Library*

BELOW: One of the later Class V1 2-6-2Ts, No 425, waits to leave North Berwick with an Edinburgh Waverley train on August 25, 1939. These three-cylinder tanks were introduced in 1930 and numbered 92 engines. The final 10 were built with higher pressure boilers, becoming Class V3, and many of the earlier engines were later fitted with these boilers. *E R Wethersett, Ian Allan Library*

BELOW: Gresley Class K4 three-cylinder 2-6-0 No 3442 *The Great Marquess* takes water at Crianlarich with the 12.5 pm Mallaig-Glasgow Queen Street train in August 1938. This class was designed specially for use on the West Highland line and used the same cylinders and motion as the Class K3 Moguls. The six engines were built at Darlington, the first in 1937 and the remainder the following year. *T G Hepburn*

BANTAM COCK
N E
3401

ABOVE: Gresley Class V2 three-cylinder 2-6-2 No 4771 *Green Arrow* roars past New Barnet with the down "Scotch Goods", the 3.35 pm Kings Cross-Niddrie express freight on July 16, 1937. No fewer than 184 of these versatile engines were built between 1936 and 1944. The name *Green Arrow* was derived from the then newly-introduced registered goods service, which used the name and symbol of a green arrow. *J P Wilson*

UPPER LEFT: Gresley's last steam locomotive design was the lightweight Class V4 three-cylinder 2-6-2 introduced in 1941. Only two engines were built and the first, No 3401 *Bantam Cock*, is seen in wartime livery at Eastfield shed on July 27, 1946. *E R Wethersett, Ian Allan Library*

LOWER LEFT: A post-war view of Class V2 2-6-2 No 823 (pre-1946 No 4794) leaving Welwyn North Tunnel with an evening Kings Cross-Leeds express in 1947. *F R Hebron*

ABOVE: Thompson Class B1 4-6-0 No 1151 blasts its way out of Sherwood Rise Tunnel on the exit from Nottingham with the 3.20 pm Marylebone-Manchester express on June 26, 1947. In the eleven years from 1942-52 a total of 410 of these general utility 4-6-0s were built, replacing many of the surviving pre-grouping express engines used on secondary passenger work. *T G Hepburn*

UPPER RIGHT: In 1945-49 10 of the Gresley Class B17 4-6-0s were rebuilt to the design of Edward Thompson with the B1-type boiler and two cylinders. The first engine rebuilt to Class B2 was No 2871 *Manchester City* and it is seen here at Kings Cross on May 20, 1946 with its 1946 number 1671 and renamed *Royal Sovereign* for working the Royal trains to and from Wolferton, replacing the two Royal 'Clauds' at Cambridge. *E R Wethersett, Ian Allan Library*

LOWER RIGHT: In 1945 Thompson's mixed traffic Class L1 2-6-4T No 9000 entered service and is pictured at Gateshead on July 25, 1946. A further 99 L1s were constructed in 1948-50. *E R Wethersett, Ian Allan Library*

LNER
1671
ROYAL SOVEREIGN

LNER
9000

UPPER LEFT: 2-8-2 *Cock o'the North* is seen at Haymarket shed after being rebuilt as a Pacific of Class A2/2 in 1944. The engine carries its 1946 number 501. *P L Melvill*

CENTRE LEFT: Thompson Class A2/1 Pacific No 3697, later named *Duke of Rothesay,* at Kings Cross shed on May 11, 1946. The four engines of this class were built at Darlington in place of the final four Class V2 in 1944-45. *E R Wethersett, Ian Allan Library*

BELOW: In 1945 Thompson rebuilt the pioneer Gresley Pacific No 4470 *Great Northern* with a new 250lb sq/in boiler and three sets of valve gear in place of the Gresley conjugated arrangement. Seen here renumbered 113 at the head of the down "Yorkshire Pullman" leaving Hadley Wood North Tunnel on May 19, 1948. *M W Earley*

ABOVE: Thompson Class A2/1 three-cylinder Pacific No 507 *Highland Chieftain* (pre-1946 No 3696) makes a very smoky departure from King Cross with the 4pm Newcastle express on April 28, 1948. Smoke deflectors were fitted to these engines in 1946-48. *C C B Herbert*

RIGHT: A southbound fish train leaves Edinburgh Waverley behind Thompson Class A2/3 three-cylinder Pacific No 521 *Watling Street* on June 17, 1947. These were the final Thompson Pacifics, of which 15 were built at Doncaster in 1946-47. *C C B Herbert*

ABOVE: In 1948 A H Peppercorn introduced the final version of the traditional LNER three-cylinder Pacific with his Class A1. Here No 60133 *Pommern* darkens the sky as it climbs from Copenhagen Tunnel with the 6.30 pm Kings Cross-Hull express in 1951.
F R Hebron

UPPER RIGHT: Peppercorn Class A1 No 60123 *H A Ivatt* heads the up "Queen of Scots" Pullman at Holbeck High Level on July 26, 1952. The 49 Peppercorn A1s were built in 1948-49, with 26 coming from Doncaster and the remaining 23 from Darlington. *Neville Fields*

LOWER RIGHT: The only Peppercorn Pacific to appear in LNER days was No 525 *A H Peppercorn,* the first of 15 Class A2 Pacifics built at Doncaster in 1947-48. Completed in December 1947 it is seen at Kings Cross on May 13, 1948. *E R Wethersett, Ian Allan Library*

ABOVE: The last LNER design of steam locomotive to enter service was Peppercorn's development of the solitary Thompson Class K1/1 2-6-0, which was a rebuild of Gresley Class K4 No 3445 *MacCailin Mór* with two cylinders in 1945. The 70 Peppercorn Class K1 Moguls entered service after nationalisation in 1949-50 and so never carried LNER livery. However the last survivor of the class, No 62005, has been preserved by the North Eastern Locomotive Preservation Group, who have made a fine job of restoring it to the LNER livery and number that it might have received. It is seen here as LNER No 2005 crossing the Murk Esk at Thomasson Foss with a Grosmont-Goathland train on the North Yorkshire Moors Railway, May 28, 1974. *John Hunt*

RIGHT: After the war in 1946 the LNER purchased a total of 200 Riddles WD Austerity 2-8-0s, which became LNER Class O7. Here WD No 77496, later LNER No 3118 and BR No 90439, labours past New Southgate with a down goods train in 1947.
F R Hebron

BELOW: The LNER also purchased 75 WD 0-6-0STs from the Ministry of Supply in 1946-47, becoming LNER Class J94. No 8059 is seen at Blaydon shed in company with a WD 2-8-0 on April 18, 1949.
J G Dewing

Rolling Stock

UPPER LEFT: Gresley third-class open coach No 61705 built in 1929 for service on the GE Section. *Ian Allan Library*

CENTRE LEFT: The interior of the third-class open coach illustrated above. This was one of the earlier LNER coaches to have doors at the ends only. *Ian Allan Library*

BELOW: In 1932 buffet cars with tubular steel chairs were introduced on the Cambridge Buffet Expresses or "Beer Trains" as they were better known. The interior of one of these coaches is illustrated. *Ian Allan Library*

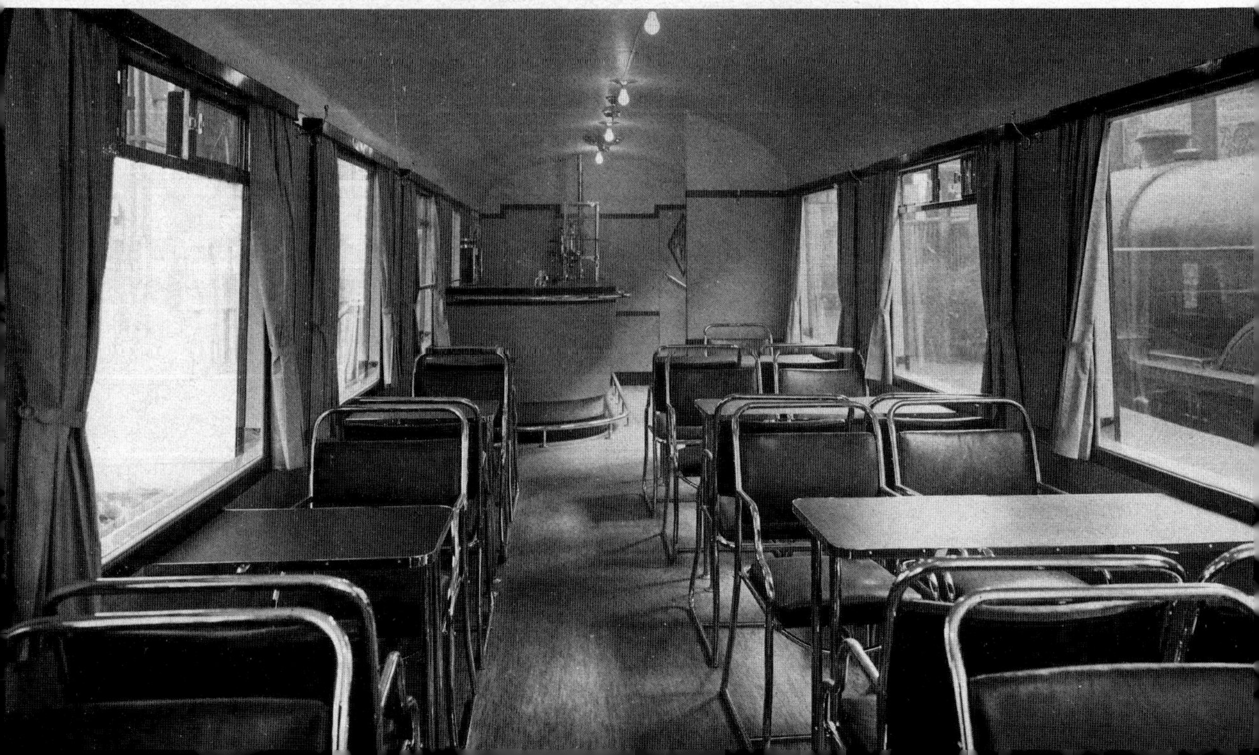

ABOVE: Passengers listen to a radio broadcast on headphones in the restaurant car of an LNER express in 1930. *Ian Allan Library*

RIGHT: A four-berth compartment in a third-class sleeping car built in 1931 for Anglo-Scottish service. *LNER, Ian Allan Library*

ABOVE: For its prestige trains the LNER built some exceedingly fine coaching stock, the comfort of which will probably never be surpassed. Illustrated here is the interior of a first class coach built at York in 1938 for the 'Hook Continental' train. *LNER, Ian Allan Library*

LEFT: Also built in 1938 at Doncaster, the interior of a buffet car for the "Flying Scotsman". Note the side corridor partitioned off. *Ian Allan Library*

UPPER RIGHT: First class coach built at York in 1937 for the "East Anglian" express introduced on September 27 that year. Meals were served at passengers seats on this train. *Ian Allan Library*

LOWER RIGHT: A first-class saloon from the 1938 "Flying Scotsman" sets. Despite their modern internal appearance these coaches were still finished externally in the traditional varnished teak. *BR*

ABOVE: One of the Sentinel 100hp six-cylinder steam railcars introduced in 1928, No 45 *Commerce* is seen at Nottingham Victoria after arrival from Pinxton when still quite new. *T G Hepburn*

BELOW: In 1934 the LNER took into stock three 250hp diesel-electric railcars built by Armstrong-Whitworth. One of these, *Lady Hamilton,* is seen at Hertford North. *Fox Photos*

ABOVE: A train of NER electric stock departs from Pelaw on a South Tyneside working about 1947. The LNER electrified the Newcastle-South Shields line in 1938. *W Hubert Foster*

BELOW: A North Tyneside electric train waits to leave Newcastle Central about 1947 formed of the two-car articulated units built by Metropolitan-Cammell in1937. *W Hubert Foster*

ABOVE: 50ton bogie sulphate wagon No 164786 built by R Y Pickering of Wishaw in 1930. *Ian Allan Library*

LEFT: Six-wheel container truck No 203878 built in 1937 for ICI traffic from Haverton Hill, near Billingham. *LNER, Ian Allan Library*

BELOW: NER 70ton WELTROL-K well wagon No 2907 loaded with a high-pressure converter at the Vickers works, Sheffield in August 1938. *English Steel Corporation Ltd*

ABOVE: 40ton bogie QUINT quintuple bolster wagon No 159657 built in 1930 by R Y Pickering & Co Ltd. *Ian Allan Library*

RIGHT: LNER 10ton large cattle truck No 153516 built in 1928. *Ian Allan Library*

BELOW: Singwriters lettering 12ton wagons at Faverdale works, Darlington about 1929. *Sport & General*

L.N.E.R.
ABERDEEN
L N E R
20

CORATOR
95
BY APPOINTMENT
TO H.M. THE KING
& Co ESTD 99 1834
COAL ME
OFFICE
L N E R
256

UPPER LEFT: A Thornycroft type B6 32 seat single-deck bus purchased in 1928 for use on the Ballater-Braemar and Huntley, Aberdeen and Banff services.

LOWER LEFT: A Strachen-bodied horse box on a Morris Commercial "Viceroy" chassis purchased in 1931. *Sport & General*

RIGHT: Two of a large number of Dennis 30cwt lorries supplied in 1931, this pair having a flat body and a detachable 'tilt' body. *Dennis Brothers Ltd*

BELOW: One of six Thornycroft type A1 vehicles supplied about 1929, two having bodies as this and the others with 20-seat omnibus bodies. *Thornycroft*

Road Vehicles

UPPER LEFT: An Albion 4ton overtype lorry purchased in 1931 is seen in the High Street Goods Station, Glasgow loaded with barrels of red wine. *Albion Motors Ltd*

CENTRE LEFT: In 1937 the LNER purchased a number of these remarkably modern-looking Thornycorft ''Sturdy'' 4-tonners. *Thorneycroft*

BELOW: A Morris Commercial 5ton "Courier" platform lorry being loaded with a container at Kings Cross Goods Yard in the mid 1930s.

ABOVE: For use on their country parcels collection and delivery service the LNER used many of these Austin 10cwt vans. Six are lined up here in 1933 for the official photographer alongside Bootham Bar, York. *LNER,*

CENTRE RIGHT: One of a fleet of 8hp Ford vans purchased in 1934 for use in the Edinburgh and Manchester districts by the bill-posting staff is photographed at Marylebone Station. *Topical Press*

LOWER RIGHT: As an alternative fuel to petrol the battery-electric vehicle became popular during World War II, and the LNER used many of these Brush 18/22cwt vans on parcels service in London and other large cities. *Brush*

Preserved LNER Engines

The preserved Gresley Class A4 Pacific No 4498 *Sir Nigel Gresley* streaks through the cutting between Dent Head and Arten Gill Viaducts on the former Midland Settle and Carlisle line with an A4 Locomotive Society special from Leeds to Carlisle on August 27, 1967. This was the 100th Gresley Pacific when built at Doncaster in 1937. *Brian Stephenson*

4472
Which way will the ball
READ THE
FINANCIAL

LEFT: A3 Pacific No 4472 *Flying Scotsman* was purchased by Mr Alan Pegler in 1963 and restored to LNER livery. Seen at Kings Cross on a special from York on August 30, 1964. It has since made a tour of the USA and Canada and is now owned by Mr W H McAlpine. *Brian Stephenson*

ABOVE: A special train from Leeds to Darlington passes Pannal hauled by the preserved Gresley Class K4 Mogul No 3442 *The Great Marquess* on October 3, 1964. No 3442 is owned by Lord Garnock *Brian Stephenson*

RIGHT: Officially preserved by BR, Class V2 Prairie No 4771 *Green Arrow* heading north from Oxford on the GWR Birmingham Line with an LCGB special on July 1, 1973. *Brian Stephenson*

Bridges

LEFT: Gresley Class P2 Mikado No 2001 *Cock o'the North* crosses the mighty Forth Bridge with an Aberdeen-Edinburgh express about 1935. *Fox Photos*

BELOW: The up "Coronation" express with its beaver tail observation car crosses the Royal Border Bridge on August 22, 1939. *E R Wethersett, Ian Allan Library*

UPPER RIGHT: A Reid NBR Class C11 Atlantic crosses the Tay Bridge from Dundee to Wormit with a southbound express about 1930. *Sport & General*

LOWER RIGHT: The up "Flying Scotsman" crosses Croxdale Viaduct, south of Durham behind Class A1 Pacific No 2564 *Knight of the Thistle* in 1929. *Fox Photos*

L N E R

Signalling

LEFT: A typical NER slotted post distant signal at Milford Junction on the Knottingley-Church Fenton line photographed on April 24, 1955. Note the old rails used to support the base of this signal. Rotten posts were often the downfall of many fine old signals. *J P Wilson*

BELOW: A set of rather unkempt GNR somersault signals at Waltham-on-the-Wold on the ironstone branch from Scalford in Leicestershire. *T G Hepburn.*

UPPER RIGHT: W Worsdell NER Class C6 Atlantic No 1792 passes under a gantry of NER slotted posted signals as it leaves York with an express for Leeds on July 19, 1938. *J P Wilson*

LOWER RIGHT: One of the loneliest signalboxes on the LNER must have been the former NBR box at Whitrope Siding on the now closed Waverley route. The photograph was taken from the down "Waverley" express in BR days. *T G Hepburn*

WHITROPE SIDING

An NBR home and distant signal stand guard against the evening sky at Tay Bridge South on July 19, 1949. *Gavin L Wilson*